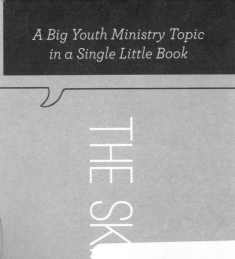

*A Big Youth Ministry Topic
in a Single Little Book*

THE SKINNY

ON

COMMUNICATION

Jeff White
with *Jeffrey Wallace*

JESUS–
CENTERED

Guide your entire ministry
toward a passionate
Jesus-centered focus with
this series of innovative
resources. Harness the
power of these dynamic
tools that will help you draw
teenagers and leaders into a
closer orbit around Jesus.

The Skinny on Communication
© 2015 Jeff White

group.com
simplyyouthministry.com

Credits
Authors: Jeff White with Jeffrey Wallace
Executive Developer: Tim Gilmour
Executive Editor: Rick Lawrence
Chief Creative Officer: Joani Schultz
Editor: Rob Cunningham
Art Director and Cover Art: Veronica Preston
Cover Photography: Rodney Stewart
Production: Joyce Douglas
Project Manager: Stephanie Krajec

Scripture quotations are taken from the Holy Bible, New Living Translation,
copyright © 1996, 2004, 2007, 2013 by Tyndale House Foundation. Used by
permission of Tyndale House Publishers, Inc., Carol Stream, Illinois 60188. All
rights reserved.

Any website addresses included in this book are offered only as a resource and/or
reference for the reader. The inclusion of these websites are not intended, in any
way, to be interpreted as an endorsement of these sites or their content on the part of
Group Publishing or the author. In addition, the author and Group Publishing do not
vouch for the content of these websites for the life of this book.

ISBN 978-1-4707-2543-3
10 9 8 7 6 5 4 3 2 1   21 20 19 18 17 16 15

Printed in the United States of America.

ACKNOWLEDGMENTS

There are always far too many people to thank for their roles in helping me create a project like this. Even the little things matter—those forgotten moments that didn't end up in a photo album but certainly helped shape who I am and what I've learned. I'm grateful for them all, and I hope I've remembered to thank them personally whenever they've left their imprint in my life.

Two people, in particular, have done more to influence my life than any others (outside of family and best friends). Thom and Joani Schultz mean the world to me, having been leaders, coaches, mentors, and true friends for more than 15 years. I wouldn't be who I am today without them, and I am eternally thankful for their unending positive impact. And when it comes to the skills of communication, you couldn't ask for better teachers and examples than Thom and Joani.

I'm also forever grateful to my wife, Amy, who has supported me for far more years than I deserve. If there's ever been a place I've failed the most at communication, it's at home. Her love, patience, and anger have been the forces that have made me a better (though far from perfect) communicator.

— Jeff White

THE SKINNY

ON

COMMUNICATION

CONTENTS

THE SKINNY

ON

COMMUNICATION

BEFORE YOU GET STARTED

The book you're holding might be "skinny," but that's because it's all-muscle. This means that Jeff White and Jeffrey Wallace have cut away the fat and focused on the "first things" that make communication in youth ministry powerful and long-lasting. In our Skinny Books series, we've paired a thought leader (in this case, Jeff White) with a master practitioner (in this case, Jeffrey Wallace) as a one-two punch. We want you to be challenged and equipped in both your thinking and your doing.

And, as a bonus, we've added an Introduction written by Thom and Joani Schultz that explores communication through the filter of a Jesus-centered approach to ministry. Jesus-centered is much more than a catchphrase to us—it's a passionate and transformative approach to life and ministry. Thom and Joani's Introduction to communication first appeared in my book *Jesus-Centered Youth Ministry,* and we couldn't think of a better way to kick off this little book. It's time to get skinny...

—RICK LAWRENCE
Executive Editor of Group Magazine

THE SKINNY ON

COMMUNICATION

INTRODUCTION

What do people mean when they call someone a "great communicator"? Generally, they mean the admired youth pastor delivers polished lectures, keeps an audience's attention for a period of time, and often hears "I really enjoyed your talk." In short, a "great communicator" is an entertainer. Entertainment is a nice thing, but is it the goal of a Jesus-centered youth ministry? Did Jesus' ministry hinge on today's definition of a "great communicator"?

We think not. In fact, the youth ministry world has been sold a lie, though with good intentions. Many youth workers look longingly at the higher profile of their senior pastors and conclude that ministry success looks like a riveting speaker. But that's not Jesus-centered ministry. That's a ministry model borrowed from the entertainment world— and the academic world. In the centuries following Jesus' ministry, the keepers of the church began to view faith as a subject to be mastered, much like any other subject such as literature or history. So, the thinking went, if we have a subject to teach, we need a studious professor to lecture rows of passive students.

The trouble is, faith in Jesus is not a subject to be mastered. Faith is a relationship. And the goal of a great relationship is an ever-deepening love, trust, and commitment to one another that demonstrates itself through self-sacrifice.

Jesus sometimes communicated truths in front of a crowd. He also mentored one-to-one, led a small group, told stories, used visual aids, challenged his friends with tough questions, and led his people through highly memorable experiences in order to cement the relationship. For our own communication to be truly effective and life-changing, it must pattern itself after Jesus. And he was a R.E.A.L. communicator—Relational, Experiential, Applicable, and Learner-based.

- **Relational.** Communication (and relationship) is greatly enhanced when everyone gets to talk.

- **Experiential.** People learn—and change—by doing. That's why Jesus used so many memorable experiences: washing the disciples' feet, calming a storm, mixing spit in the dirt to make a healing mud, and so on.

- **Applicable.** Our communication should give young people a clear idea of how to live out today's message in everyday life.

- **Learner-based.** It's not about you. It's about your kids—and their relationship with Jesus. Just as Jesus did, we need to adapt our approach to how our teenagers will most effectively be reached.

Effective communication in ministry looks a lot like the kinds of communicating found in a healthy friendship.

—Thom Schultz, *Founder and CEO of Group Publishing*
—Joani Schultz, *Chief Creative Officer of Group Publishing*

CHAPTER

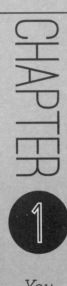

1

You

Cannot

NOT

Communicate

THE SKINNY

ON

COMMUNICATION

You've seen this before:

A mother and young son sit down to eat together at a fast-food restaurant. It starts out with smiles and anticipation. She squirts some ketchup on a napkin for the kid's fries while the boy sticks his straw in his drink. The 5-year-old talks animatedly about how excited he is to open his meal toy, while his mom unwraps her sandwich. They're both happy to be together. But before the fries even have a chance to get cold, their encounter changes.

The mother pulls out her phone.

From that point forward, the conversation is reduced to a scattering of "mm-hm's" and "yeps" from the mom while the boy's chatter eventually fades to silence.

Most might assume that, in this moment, the mother stopped communicating with her son. But that couldn't be further from the truth. Whether she meant to or not, the woman sent some very clear messages to her child: "This phone is more important than you. I don't want to talk to you. I'm happy to sit with you, but I'm going to mostly ignore you." You couldn't blame the kid for hearing any of those messages, even though they weren't said out loud.

Intended or not, the mom communicated clearly to her child without saying a word.

This book isn't about the pitfalls of modern technology. Nor is it about parenting. It's about the importance of communication, and how just about everything you do and say sends a message to the people around you.

I could list a million different scenarios that demonstrate the principle of communication not having an "off" button:

- A young couple at the end of their first date. The man says he really looks forward to seeing her again. She changes the subject and begins talking about how delicious the dinner was.

- A homeless man sits on the sidewalk, his cup of nickels held out in shame. People avoid eye contact as they quicken their pace.

- A boss asks a room of employees who would like to take on the next assignment. Everyone stares into their laps. No words are spoken, but the message is clear.

We all do it every day, often without giving it any thought. We cannot *not* communicate. When others try to send us messages, we always send a message back, whether we intend it or not.

We don't know anyone who communicates too much, or too well. Every one of us could list at least one communication shortcoming for each of our closest friends. We *all* have improvements to make—and we *always* will. This book is meant to help you as a leader and a youth worker.

FOCUS OVER FORMULA

I'm not a fan of formulas. I don't believe in (or fall for) five-step plans that will solve your problems. I don't buy into the thinking that a universal set of rules will cure all your communication ills. And I'm certainly not naïve enough to think that every person reading this book is going to soak up and apply everything and become a master communicator.

I do know, however, that focusing on specific principles can move us closer toward mastering a skill like communication. I also know that there will be a handful of points in this book that will stand out to you and cause you to change your behavior, if at least a little.

Grab a highlighter and mark whatever makes you furrow your eyebrows, narrow your eyes, and say "Hmm."

This book would be worthless if you found yourself just nodding in agreement and thinking, "Oh, yeah, I already do all that stuff." (I can assure you that you don't.) You'll have opportunities here and there to try a few things out and see if they work. Challenge yourself to be wrong once or twice or a dozen times. Allow yourself to be surprised.

I also believe that any nonfiction book worth reading should do two things:

1. Tell you something you haven't heard before ("I did not know that")

2. Challenge you to rethink your assumptions and give you a fresh perspective ("I never thought of it that way before")

I don't expect you to agree with everything I've written here, but I hope you'll grapple with a lot of it and allow yourself to try a few new things.

The artist James Christensen said, "Different isn't always better, but the same is never better."[1]

We're here to try something different.

❷ A YOUTH WORKER'S PERSPECTIVE *Jeffrey Wallace*

In general, people don't process information the same, and there is not just one "cookie cutter" principle that will teach you how to effectively engage and communicate with every teenager. The purpose of this book is to challenge you and stretch you to reach beyond your comfort zone. This generation of young people sees the world with a highly eclectic lens. With that in mind, it is vital for you as an influencer and a voice speaking into the life of this youth culture to expand your insight, concepts, ideas, and practices for being an efficient and effective communicator.

THE PURPOSE OF COMMUNICATION IN YOUTH MINISTRY

Before jumping into the practices and principles of effective communication, it would be worthwhile to qualify it all with a premise. What's our goal?

Communication principles are generally universal—that is, they apply to the majority of people in the majority of situations. (There are always exceptions, of course.) However, this book is about communication in youth ministry and the unique challenges and opportunities along our path.

The purpose of effective communication in youth ministry is based on one primary idea:

Faith is a relationship.

Stop and think about that for a moment. *Faith is a relationship.* It's not a topic to be studied. It's not a checklist of things to do. It's not something ethereal or intangible. Faith is all about a relationship—our relationship with Jesus and with each other.

When the religious leaders asked Jesus to name the most important commandment, Jesus started by saying that it was to love God with all your heart, soul, mind, and strength. But he didn't stop there. Jesus also said, "The second is equally important: 'Love your neighbor as yourself' " (Mark 12:28-31).

Jesus said, above all else, we must put loving God AND loving others first. They're equally important, according to Christ.

That's why healthy, effective communication is so critical in youth ministry. Our most significant responsibility—arguably our ONLY responsibility—is to love God and love teens (as well as their parents, our volunteers, and our fellow church leaders). That's nothing if not relational. And communication is the fuel for any relationship. We love people through our actions, our words, our attitudes, our facial expressions, and every other way we communicate.

First Corinthians 13 proves it. Every characteristic of love mentioned in that profound chapter involves communication.

The opposite is true, as well: We communicate our *lack* of love through our actions, words, attitudes, expressions, and every other form of communication.

So we can say, "I love you" and "God loves you" as much as we want, but unless we communicate it through our whole being, it means nothing.

If you want to fulfill your calling and make the most of your ministry, learning to communicate love effectively must be at the top of your priority list.

Far too often, we think having a "catchy" topic and using slang and youthful jargons are the most necessary methods of engaging teenagers when it comes to communicating with them. That is not always true. You've likely heard the age-old saying, "People don't care how much you know until they know how much you care." More than your fancy titles, young people connect with communicators who love them and who live authentically before them. When teenagers know you love them, they will listen to anything you have to say. For a lot of young people, especially those who are coming from unhealthy home environments, it is the simple things, like love, that matter most.

"Communication is a path, not an event."
— AUTHOR AND ENTREPRENEUR SETH GODIN[2]

THE ASYMPTOTE

If you remember your high school geometry classes, you might recall a word called "asymptote." An asymptote is a line that continuously approaches a curved line—but never touches it.

The majority of church ministry today is asymptotic. It goes on and on, year after year, but never actually connects with the people it's aiming for. The asymptote of ministry does a lot of preaching, a lot of teaching, a lot of singing, a lot of Bible studies—a whole lot of one-way communication—but doesn't ever get close enough to form a relational bond. For a while it may appear as though we're running parallel, but in reality there's no connection. We miss the curve.

The lines of love never touch.

Fortunately, our ministries can avoid this problem (and be "nonasymptotic," if you like fancy words). The solution for the asymptote in ministry is actually quite simple: **frequent, continual, two-way communication.** The lines touch, the connections are made, and relationships happen.

WHAT TEENAGERS NEED

Not only could I list a million reasons teenagers tend to shy away from church, I could also list a million different things kids say they want and need in their lives. It could melt your brain if you try to create a strategy that addresses the countless ways you can impact their lives. This book is designed to prevent brain melting.

Researchers George Gallup and Dr. Michael Lindsay conducted an extensive study[3] to learn what Americans really wanted out of church. While their research involved mostly adults, I've found the results hold just as true for teens. They uncovered six basic needs:

- The need to believe life is meaningful and has a purpose

- The need for a sense of community and deeper relationships

- The need to be listened to and be heard

- The need to feel one is growing in faith

- The need to be appreciated and respected

- The need for practical help in developing a mature faith

Now, what teenager wouldn't be attracted to a ministry that delivered on those needs?

Not surprisingly, communication plays a foundational role in meeting each one of these areas. In fact, it's impossible to meet these needs without effective communication. And the more effective you are at communicating, the better able you'll be to give teens exactly what they're looking for in a church experience.

The bulk of this book will do just that.

THE THREE FUNDAMENTALS OF EFFECTIVE COMMUNICATION

I did a Google search for the word *communication* and got about 1,080,000,000 results (that's more than a BILLION, by the way). I'm kind of surprised it wasn't more. There are perhaps an infinite number of different ways to approach effective communication, and it seems as though all the experts have different theories. Psychologists, public speakers, business pros, salespeople, coaches, teachers, entertainers, ministers, and everyone else's aunt and uncle have something to say about what it takes to be an effective communicator.

So where does one start?

My favorite and most useful source takes us back more than 2,000 years ago to a fellow named Aristotle. His breakdown of the basics gets us to the core of communication in a very simple way, and it's just as relevant today as ever.

In his classic work *Rhetoric*, Aristotle cites the three essential elements of good communication: *ethos, pathos,* and *logos.*[4]

Ethos refers to your character and values as a person, a leader, and a church. It's essentially about your credibility. Do people know what you believe? Do they know what you stand for? Do they think you know what you're talking about? Do they perceive you as believable?

Pathos refers to connecting with people emotionally. Will people relate to you? Do they feel a personal bond with you? Studies have shown this to be the most powerful of the three elements, but it also has the greatest potential for misuse and mistakes.

Logos refers to your words or message. It appeals to people's logical side. What are you trying to say? What are your facts, your conclusions? While *logos* is essential to good communication, it never works on its own. As nice as it would be simply to say a truth and have people believe it, it rarely—pretty much never—works that way.

As we explore principles and strategies for communication in ministry throughout this book, we'll refer to *ethos, pathos,* and *logos* to make sure we're on track with the three basics.

As you establish and refine your communication strategy in your ministry, you'll need to address all three of these elements. The more you can improve in all three, the more effective you'll be in your communication. I've included a handy worksheet here to help you get started in discovering how *ethos, pathos,* and *logos* play a role in your ministry.

List the top three values of your youth ministry, and why you think teenagers would care about each one personally (be realistic):

* _____

* _____

* _____

If teens were to describe your ministry to a peer, what three things would they say about it?

* _____

* _____

* _____

Why would (or wouldn't) teenagers say they can trust what you tell them?

Would the kids in your youth group say you care about them personally? Why would (or wouldn't) they say that?

What are three things teenagers would say they have in common with you?

*   _____

*   _____

*   _____

Aside from occasional one-on-one time, what are two or three things you do to build a personal bond with the kids in your youth group?

*   _____

*   _____

*   _____

What are three things you want every kid in your group to know?

- _____

- _____

- _____

Besides lecture, what are two or three ways your teens spend time learning your "content"? Which method would they say is most effective?

- _____

- _____

- _____

What would the teenagers in your youth group say you talk about the most? How much would they say they remember from your times together?

❯ A YOUTH WORKER'S PERSPECTIVE Jeffrey Wallace

Effective communication often requires a strategy that has a hybrid of all three of these elements. I teach my team at my church that as a leader, I am looking for people who (1) have Christ-like character, (2) have great chemistry with other leaders and our teenagers, and (3) are competent when it comes to their understanding of God's Word and their ability to communicate it clearly to others.

THE SKINNY ON

COMMUNICATION

CHAPTER 2

*Four Surprising
Communication
Strategies That
Totally Work*

THE SKINNY

ON

COMMUNICATION

General communication principles tend to be universal.

Whether I say "Hi!" to someone at work, in my neighborhood, in the supermarket, or at church, the same rules apply pretty much everywhere. We interpret the same common facial expressions and we expect similar kinds of responses. Of course, the closer those relationships are, the richer those communication experiences can be.

There are any number of communication resources you could read to help you be a more effective communicator. This book, however, is specifically for communication in youth ministry. So rather than give you tips you could apply anywhere, this portion of the book will cover four unique communication strategies specially designed for Christian ministry. We'll explore how they will help you communicate effectively with teenagers, parents, and other partners in your ministry. As a result, you'll find that these aren't simply communication strategies, but are *ministry strategies that are rooted in and practiced through effective communication.*

With Thom and Joani Schultz's book *Why Nobody Wants to Go to Church Anymore: And How Four Acts of Love Will Make Your Church Irresistible* as a major inspiration, we're going to dig into four communication strategies that parallel those four acts of love. They're brilliant, and they really work. These acts of love are full manifestations of healthy communication. You can think about it two ways:

1. Ministering to people through these four strategies will make you an outstanding communicator

2. Communicating to people using these four strategies will make your ministry outstanding

The four communication strategies are:

- Radical Hospitality

- Fearless Conversation

- Genuine Humility

- Divine Anticipation

I'll provide practical applications to each strategy aimed at teens and parents. (By the way, these strategies work for your volunteers and fellow church leaders, too.) We'll also see how *ethos, pathos,* and *logos* make these techniques so effective as communication tools.

One quick personal note before we jump into the strategies: Can we please stop referring to the kids in our youth groups as "students"? The word *student* is an academic term that implies a primary role of learning and studying. Will teens learn stuff? Of course. Is that the main reason they're part of your group? I sure hope not.

What do teenagers really need most in a youth ministry? They need to be loved, as well as given the opportunity to love God and others (Mark 12:28-31). When you use the following four communication strategies to love the kids in your ministry, you'll see a dramatic impact in how their lives are touched by your efforts and God's love.

⊙ A YOUTH WORKER'S PERSPECTIVE *Jeffrey Wallace*

As a youth leader, always remember that you function as a secondary influencer—the parent or guardian being the primary—when it comes to the spiritual formation of the life of a teenager. Your ability to effectively communicate God's love and purpose has a profound effect on the development of a teenager's Jesus-centered worldview.

Let's go!

One of the teachers of religious law was standing there listening to the debate. He realized that Jesus had answered well, so he asked, "Of all the commandments, which is the most important?" Jesus replied, "The most important commandment is this: 'Listen, O Israel! The Lord our God is the one and only Lord. And you must love the Lord your God with all your heart, all your soul, all your mind, and all your strength.' The second is equally important: 'Love your neighbor as yourself.' No other commandment is greater than these."

(MARK 12:28-31)

MINISTRY COMMUNICATION STRATEGY #1: RADICAL HOSPITALITY

"You're welcome just as you are."

Many churches say that, but do they really mean it? Do our churches reach the same kinds of people Jesus embraced? The cheaters and liars, the despised and rejected, the stinky and dirty, the partiers and moochers? The religious leaders didn't like it, but for Jesus it was a priority. He didn't expect people to clean themselves up and get their act together *before* he could build a relationship.

When it came to meeting people, "Let's chat" was Jesus' unspoken motto.

Radical hospitality is a fundamental act of communication—a path to relationship. It's simply welcoming others and being glad to be with them. It's not our job or even our "ministry." It's born out of a Spirit-led desire to love people.

In my youth group, it is mandatory for leaders to help create an environment where our teenagers know that we were expecting them and that we are glad they're here. Radical hospitality is essential when it comes to communicating love to young people. If your youth room is dirty, your leaders are late, no one speaks to new or regular participants, and you just "wing it" from week to week, you are fooling yourself to expect that young people will want to build and cultivate a relationship with you and your team— or believe that you actually care about them.

It's relationally authentic, just as our communication should be. We don't have an agenda. And we should never approach a teenager as something that needs fixing. We simply care. We're curious about young people and who they really are. They can always tell when you view them as a "project."

When we show radical hospitality to teenagers, parents, and volunteers, we're communicating to them, loudly and clearly, that we accept them, no matter what. Seriously— no matter what. Their personality, attitude, appearance, economic status, and anything else that makes them unique, shouldn't make a lick of difference. We accept them, and we let them know it. And we do it, by the way, without qualifying judgments, such as, "I accept you in spite of _____." God made them, God loves them, and so should we.

Radical hospitality is deeply personal, and NOT a handful of outreach tactics. It's not just greeting teens with a smile at the door. It's not a meet-and-greet icebreaker that gives them a couple of minutes to swap names. It's not the bait you use to get kids to attend. It's not drinks and snacks (although, when accompanied with friendly people, those can be a useful tool).

There's nothing wrong with any of those things; in fact, they're often worth doing. Just don't mistake them for true radical hospitality and its potential for more meaningful connections with teens.

Undoubtedly, this approach to communication and relationships can be messy and uncomfortable. The limits of our patience and perseverance will be tested. But that's what love is for, yes?

Here are some *ethos/pathos/logos* tips for using radical hospitality as a communication strategy with teenagers:

Ethos

- **Learn and use names.** We all love to hear our names, and it makes us feel known and accepted. Make a continual, concerted effort to use everyone's names and to make sure everybody in your group knows each other's names. It's empowering. And if you think about it, using people's names makes you something of an expert about them as individuals. It's a surefire credibility booster.

❍ A YOUTH WORKER'S PERSPECTIVE Jeffrey Wallace

Try to learn two or three new names per week. And during your initial conversation, repeat the teenager's name at least two or three times.

- **Rely on word of mouth.** There's nothing radically hospitable about marketing and manufactured hype and mass communication. When your approach to relationships is genuine, teens will embrace it and find you to be a credible leader. And when your youth have legitimate reasons to tell their friends about the

cool things going on in your ministry, they will,
naturally. They'll tell their friends and bring
them to your group.

❍ A YOUTH WORKER'S PERSPECTIVE *Jeffrey Wallace*

*Teenagers are the greatest marketing tools you will ever
need when it comes to promoting your youth group and your
program. If your young people believe in and are proud of
your program, they will strongly encourage others to join.*

Pathos

- **Build friendships first.** If you don't make a
  personal, emotional connection with each
  person in your ministry, you'll never—*never*—be
  able to communicate with them effectively.
  By showing them radical hospitality, you're
  proving to them that you care about your
  relationship above all else.

- **Be intentional in your relationships.** This
  doesn't just happen because you're in the same
  room every week. Your deliberate effort in
  bonding with them will feel radical to teenagers
  in today's world, where such attempts at
  authentic relationships are rare. Fully engaged,
  face-to-face time is always best. (And it doesn't
  always have to be one-on-one, either.)

Logos

- **Watch your language.** Our Christian jargon
  and churchy code words can leave young people
  in the dark. Words and phrases that may seem
  second nature to us can confuse teens or make
  them feel like outsiders. We're never going to
  impress them with our extensive theological
  vocabularies. Our messages will never be
  communicated clearly if we don't speak a
  common language.

❯ A YOUTH WORKER'S PERSPECTIVE *Jeffrey Wallace*

*Unchurched teenagers, in particular, already think church
people are weird. Never communicate in a way that only
makes sense to just you. I intentionally have a group of
student leaders who are my "ears in the streets." They give
me "street cred" by keeping me informed on what's going
on, what I should say, and what I shouldn't say. I empower
these leaders to help me stay informed on how our young
people are tracking, connecting, engaging, and growing
spiritually.*

- **Use storytelling as the basis for your message.** Not just your stories, but everyone's. The more teenagers get the opportunity to add their stories to your group's *logos*, the more they feel an integral part of the community. They'll own the message if they're an intrinsic part of it.

- **Keep it simple.** Make fewer points. Purge the noise. Make room for simple and honest responses. We all know far too many people who love to hear themselves talk. Resist the urge to say more than necessary.

"Unlike sharing, where the group is mainly an aggregate of participants, cooperating creates group identity."
— CLAY SHIRKY, *HERE COMES EVERYBODY: THE POWER OF ORGANIZING WITHOUT ORGANIZATIONS*[5]

RADICAL HOSPITALITY STRATEGIES FOR PARENTS

Parents are funny creatures. And by funny I mean not really very funny. They want the best of both worlds: They want youth ministers to be a (if not THE) major influence in shaping their kids' spiritual lives, yet they simultaneously may seem to do everything they can to thwart those efforts.

Most parents feel they need all the help they can get when it comes to guiding their teens through those impressionable years. Whether their expectations are sky-high or nonexistent, your communication through radical hospitality can make all the difference.

Here are a few *ethos, pathos,* and *logos* tips for communicating to parents through radical hospitality:

Ethos

- **Find common ground.** Build your personal relationships with parents by discovering shared values. Moms and dads need to know you're on the same page, even if it's only regarding "minor" issues. If parents see you taking the time to know them, they'll perceive that the same thing must be happening with their children.

Pathos

- **Prove that you care.** It's not enough to say it. It requires additional effort on your part, but take the time to invest in the kids' lives in visible, tangible ways (and parents' lives, too, if the opportunity arises). You'll be communicating that you're emotionally invested in their child's life, not just there to share a few Bible verses with them.

- **Tell parents good news about their kids.**
  Moms and dads LOVE to hear good things
  about their children. When you see something—
  anything—worth praising a teenager for, tell the
  parents how much you appreciate that about
  them. One small compliment can give mothers
  and fathers all the hope they need that their
  sons and daughters just might turn out OK.

Logos

- **Share your secret sauce.** Be as transparent as
  possible. Whenever you can do it face to face,
  tell parents about your approach to ministry.
  Give them the details of how you make loving
  God and others a priority. If you follow the
  four strategies of ministry communication in
  this book, explain to parents how that changes
  teenagers' hearts and lives.

➲ A YOUTH WORKER'S PERSPECTIVE *Jeffrey Wallace*

*Whether you agree or disagree with them, parents and
guardians are the primary influencers in the lives of your
teenagers. If you are going to be successful in ministry,
you must develop a comprehensive strategy that engages
parents.*

MINISTRY COMMUNICATION STRATEGY #2: FEARLESS CONVERSATION

When was the last time you thoroughly enjoyed being lectured to? That's what I thought. Teenagers don't need a lecture. No one *wants* a lecture. Lectures stink like rotten cheese.

Youth ministries—and church ministries in general— need far less one-way communication and far more fearless conversations.

❯ A YOUTH WORKER'S PERSPECTIVE *Jeffrey Wallace*

The church should always be a hospital for the hurting and the information center for the uninformed. Like it or not, your young people are exposed to so much, and they struggle with a great deal of physical, spiritual, and emotional issues: sexuality and identity issues, fatherlessness, drug abuse and addiction, social media, family dysfunctions, depression, suicidal thoughts, and so much more. When it comes to your approach to having fearless conversations, you must pray about it, be willing to be transparent with your teenagers, and always point them back to the Scriptures in a real and relevant way. As much as possible, don't build your conversations on just your own personal feelings and opinions. Always lead the conversation with Jesus-centered love, respect, and grace.

Do you welcome teens' thoughts...without needing to correct them if they disagree with you? Do you welcome hard questions...without always having good answers? Do you welcome their doubts...without feeling compelled to dismiss them? Do you welcome their curiosity...while allowing them the freedom to discover truth at their own pace?

Teenagers will listen to what we have to say...once we've proven to them that we care about what *they* have to say. Relationship precedes belief.

Jesus welcomed fearless conversations. It's rather eye-opening to see how many times Jesus started chats using provocative, open-ended questions. He often asked, "What do you think?" and he didn't always respond with a definitive answer.

Likewise, your listening ear and caring approach will allow young people to see God's love shine through you. Church isn't about getting everyone to agree and finally come around to seeing things your way. It's about loving God and others, period.

These kinds of conversations are "fearless" because we don't have anything to be afraid of. Taboos are imaginary; God is not. God is in control, and God isn't afraid of hard questions. When we trust God to be with us, there is no room for fear.

Let's take a look at some *ethos, pathos,* and *logos* communication strategies for using fearless conversation in your ministry:

Ethos

- **Redefine your role as a leader.** We live in an age when the entire world of information is literally in our hands. In seconds, we can find answers to billions of questions simply by tapping our thumbs on a tiny screen. We can become experts with little effort. As a result, the act of learning is evolving before our eyes.

  Your credibility as a leader no longer lies with how much you know, but how well you can facilitate God-connecting experiences. It requires fewer presentation abilities and more relational skills. We need to master the art of interpersonal communication. The better you can facilitate fearless conversations, the more effective your youth ministry will be.

- **Minimize one-way communication.** If only one person is doing the talking, there is no conversation. And there's certainly no *fearless* conversation. It's an effort by the leader to control all the information, rather than letting everybody participate and allowing God to work through us relationally.

When we let teenagers talk, we expand ownership of the truth. Let everyone be a teacher, since "the one who learns the most is the teacher." We've all got something to share, to contribute, to question. Let's give everyone the joy of discovering God's truth—together.

Pathos

- **Trade "studies" for "explorations."** Bible studies are designed for Bible experts. Teens, who usually aren't Bible experts, are often afraid to speak up or share during Bible studies because they may give the wrong answer. They may not know who "John" is or why he used the secret "3:16" code. And as they listen idly to veterans in the group pontificate over "deep" content, they find the Bible more intimidating. It squashes any emotional connection (*pathos*) with your message (*logos*). I've not experienced much inspiring *pathos* in most of the Bible studies I've attended over the years.

  Instead of studying the Bible academically, let's encourage conversation centered on one simple Bible truth at a time. Allow young people to talk in pairs and trios, so they won't be afraid to express what they really think or ask the confounding questions rattling their brains.

- **Encourage storytelling.** One of the best ways to make an emotional connection with someone is to hear their story. We discover the ups and downs of their journey. We understand what motivates them, what hurts them, what they yearn for in life. And by listening we show them that we value them as people.

  By the way, when someone tells their story, they've just made themselves vulnerable and shared an important part of their life. Don't trivialize it. Don't re-explain it to everyone. Don't score it ("That was such an amazing story" or "I liked everything except the part about..."). Don't gloss over it as if they didn't say anything. Don't use it as a sermon illustration. Instead, thank that person. Ask follow-up questions to dig deeper, with the sole intention of simply wanting to hear more.

Logos

- **Let teens grapple.** If the only questions we ask are the ones to which we already know the answers, that's not an authentic conversation. It's never fun for the people who aren't privy to the "right" answers. Most classes are about giving answers to questions we're not asking. Plus, it's one-way communication.

A far better approach to both communication and ministry is to let teenagers wrestle with good questions. Rather than spoon-feed information, let's facilitate vibrant conversations where everyone actively participates. Where everyone has a story to tell. Where everyone has a voice. And where everyone gets a chance to discover, firsthand, what God's love is all about.

- **No topic is off-limits.** No question is out of the question. The content we prepare for our youth groups needs to be ready for that. If kids can't bring their hardest questions to us, where are they going to take them? If they can't watch us grapple with them over tough subjects, how else will they learn the importance of dealing with those topics head-on?

"To make our communications more effective, we need to shift our thinking from 'What information do I need to convey?' to 'What questions do I want my audience to ask?'"
—CHIP HEATH AND DAN HEATH, *MADE TO STICK: WHY SOME IDEAS SURVIVE AND OTHERS DIE*[6]

➔ A YOUTH WORKER'S PERSPECTIVE *Jeffrey Wallace*

Teenagers love dialogue and interactive learning. It's been my experience that the more you can get your young people involved in the conversation or discussion, the more understanding they receive. Teenagers love to talk; they are highly opinionated, and they want to be heard. When young people start talking and they see that you aren't trying to belittle them or disregard their feelings, it becomes contagious—other kids who may normally not participate will begin to engage in the conversation as well.

A personal perspective: Don't let teenagers take you too far off the topic—that doesn't mean you have to keep strict control of the conversation, but you may need to step in and guide things at times. Communicate to your teenagers that this is a #SafeTalkZone.

FEARLESS CONVERSATION STRATEGIES FOR PARENTS

While the same principles apply, we do have different kinds of conversations with parents, as well as different objectives. The important thing to remember is that we have the opportunity to show love to parents through our communication. Here's how we can do that through fearless conversation:

Ethos

- **Invite guest experts.** As youth leaders, we're not authorities on every topic. Our opinions are just that: opinions. You can help put parents at ease with your fearless conversations by asking experts to drop in and join the conversation. If your group talks about birth control or mental health, invite specialized physicians to come and share stories and answer questions. If you tackle tough topics like racism or abuse, bring in people who've experienced it firsthand. You can increase your credibility by letting parents know that you're strengthening your fearless conversations by including those who are most credible.

Pathos

- **Affirm parents.** I've found it's usually a pleasant surprise when moms and dads hear

really good things about their kids. They spend
so much of their time frustrated and unsure
and at a loss. They feel like failures as parents
more than they'd like to admit. That's why they
need good news. Affirmation is hope made real.
And it doesn't take much to be effective: "Your
daughter asked such a great question today." "I
really admire your son's ability to grapple with
deep issues." "I had no idea your daughter was
so gifted at giving compliments." It's perhaps
the greatest gift you can give a parent. The look
of delight on their face will confirm your solid
emotional connection.

Logos

- **Explain the why.** I've heard this question a
  lot: "How could you talk about THAT in your
  youth group?" Clarify the goal of fearless
  conversation: to emulate Jesus' approach
  to tackling tough subjects head-on. Remind
  parents of the need for relevance in your
  ministry. The more you're able to link God's
  Word with topics teens are most interested
  in, the better able you'll be to keep their kids'
  engagement with God and relationships at
  church. Ultimately, you want to reassure
  parents that Jesus—the Logos, the Word—is
  always the center of your discussions.

MINISTRY COMMUNICATION STRATEGY #3: GENUINE HUMILITY

Humility as a communication strategy? Actually, as an act of love, it's an indispensable element to communication in church youth ministry. Conversely, a lack of humility is one of the greatest barriers to healthy communication.

Genuine humility is acknowledgement that we ALL fall short, that we ALL need to grow, and that, in God's eyes, we're ALL equals. It's saying I'm no better than you, that we need each other, and that we're in this together.

A loving relationship is at the root of genuine humility.

Since we have to admit that none of us is 100 percent right about everything, genuine humility asks us to be open to learning from those who believe and think differently than we do. That doesn't mean we have to believe like they do, but it does mean we listen with respect—and consider the possibility that we might be wrong.

How does genuine humility show up in the spectrum of *ethos, pathos,* and *logos* in our communication?

Ethos

- **Admit your mistakes.** I have a hard time trusting people who think they're always right. The Mr. and Mrs. Know-It-Alls of the world tend to rub me the wrong way, just as they did when I was a teenager.

  When someone admits they were wrong, it grabs our attention. As youth leaders we can be models of vulnerability. Every one of us has flaws. Isn't that why we're at church in the first place? Acknowledging our imperfections communicates our credibility more surprisingly than perhaps any other act. In many ways, it's the most relevant thing we can do in youth ministry.

- **Speak autobiographically.** You know your own story. Tell it. Don't wait until you think you have a story to tell. Tell the one you know right now. And be sure to let others tell their story, too. Those stories will be different from yours. YOU are the most credible YOU.

Pathos

- **Put people first.** This isn't to say that God is second. For one thing, Jesus said that loving others is as "equally important" as loving God (Mark 12:28-31). It's also a statement about all the other things churches tend to prioritize over people: the dispensation of Scripture, our sacred spaces, the rules and traditions they must submit to, the authority of church leadership, etc., etc., etc. When teenagers see that you care about them above all else, they'll see God's love shining through. You can't ask for more credibility than that.

Logos

- **Clear, direct communication.** Here are a few adjectives to describe the way we should communicate to every person in our church ministry: honest, direct, open, clear, transparent, and straightforward. Here are a few adjectives that describe how we should NOT communicate: secretive, manipulative, exclusive, incomplete, dishonest, malicious, and mysterious. When we have an issue, we need to go straight to the person who can do something about it. That's humble because it shows a willingness not to place ourselves above others. It's also loving because we want everyone to stay plugged in.

- **Learn from those who are different from you.**
  The Millennial generation—the generational
  label that still covers most of the kids in our
  youth ministries—will not tolerate the person
  who says there is only one right point of view.
  They are naturally open to hearing different
  perspectives. That's a great opportunity for
  you to facility dynamic conversations with
  people and perspectives that don't see eye to
  eye with you. These experiences shine a light on
  your genuine humility, and they're a powerful
  communication strategy for allowing teenagers
  to strengthen their faith.

➲ A YOUTH WORKER'S PERSPECTIVE *Jeffrey Wallace*

*When you as a leader lead in a way where you are modeling
vulnerability, putting others first, providing clear and direct
communication, and being intentional about not judging
others, it creates an environment and culture of love,
acceptance, and openness that teenagers really want and
willingly gravitate to.*

GENUINE HUMILITY STRATEGIES FOR PARENTS

Humility can go a looooooooong way with moms and dads. They find face-to-face, heart-to-heart interactions with youth leaders compelling, especially when they're grounded in friendship. Imagine the impact if your ministry had the kind of reputation that caused parents to say, "If you want a place where the leaders care about parents and what they think, this is it! You can count on them!"

Communicating through humility isn't hard, but it does take deliberate effort in your *ethos, pathos,* and *logos* strategies:

Ethos

- **Be intentional.** We're in ministry to love people. That means parents, too. My wife's a teacher. A really good one. The reason for her success? She cares about her kids and builds relationships with them. They know it, and they never doubt it, because she's completely honest with them. Her emotional connection never wavers because the kids have no doubt that she's got their best interests in mind, even when she's tough on them. Relationship comes first, and it's never an accident—particularly for moms and dads.

Pathos

- **Be inquisitive.** If a parent expresses frustration or dissatisfaction with something in your youth ministry, don't get defensive. Instead, realize that mom or dad is coming from a place of pain. So much conflict in churches these days quickly devolves into complaining, fighting, bullying, or worse. Genuine humility prevents that from happening. Ask wondering questions to uncover the parent's story. Let them share their experiences, and listen closely. You'll likely find out that the seed of their disappointment has nothing to do with your ministry. And it opens the door to ministering to them at a deep, emotional level.

Logos

- **Be clear.** All the truth in the world isn't worth a can of beans and weenies if it's not understood and received. Misunderstandings (more on that later) are inevitable, but they don't have to be unbearable. Take every opportunity to chat with parents about their kids and about your goals as a youth leader. When it's clear to parents that your ongoing goal is to love God and others, they're more likely to jump on board and paddle in the same direction.

MINISTRY COMMUNICATION STRATEGY #4: DIVINE ANTICIPATION

Jesus modeled divine anticipation throughout his ministry. He expected God to show up, and he relied on God's love and power to make a difference.

Most of the youth leaders I know are open to trying new things—perhaps more so than any other area of ministry. Yet we all have a natural tendency to stick to what we know best and are most comfortable with.

As we try new methods and strategies in our ministries, we need to be as open as possible to encountering God in ways we don't expect. We must let the Holy Spirit do the work that God intended, where each situation is taken out of our hands and is completely in God's control.

Divine anticipation is a fundamental act of communication in ministry. It isn't about hearing God's literal voice or seeing his actual face or feeling the touch of his bodily hands. Divine anticipation gives our efforts a dynamic, real-life expression of our experiences with God. It's as real as it gets.

Here's how the three elements of communication are lived out in our divine anticipation:

Ethos

- **Accepting the unexplainable.** Millennials have a lot of tough questions, and they have little patience for unsatisfying answers. Millennials are comfortable in that blurry, sometimes contradictory space. That's precisely why they value faith. They're at ease with intellectual grappling, and they embrace the gray zones. We boost our credibility with teens when we admit our limitations and say, "I don't know."

- **Understand relevance.** No youth minister wants teenagers telling their friends that their church isn't relevant in their lives. But being cool doesn't make us relevant. Having tattoos and snarky T-shirts and the latest video game system doesn't do it, either. Relevance is all about dealing with the most practical and meaningful aspects of a person's life. It's deeply personal. Relevance is not dismissing questions about things like homosexuality, poverty, or technology with a couple of Scripture verses—it's encouraging those conversations to happen and not dominating them with our own motives. If we're relevant, we're credible.

Pathos

- **Allow teens to express their faith in their own way.** The majority of traditions practiced in our churches aren't actually in the Bible. That's not to say they're unbiblical. But it does mean that our expressions of faith vary widely from denomination to denomination, church to church, family to family, and individual to individual. We don't make emotional bonds through rules, performances, and other restraints. When you allow young people the freedom to experience God in fresh ways, you're encouraging them to make stronger emotional connections with God and with you. Divine anticipation offers a deeper level of *pathos* for you and your youth.

Logos

- **Use God Sightings.** When it comes to divine anticipation, this can be one of your primary tools for helping teens see God at work all around them. When you make it a regular practice of sharing your God Sightings, as well as encouraging kids to do the same, you've opened everyone's eyes to what God is really doing. It's especially powerful because teens hear from other teens, again and again, how God is intimately involved in their daily lives. You can't ask for much better *logos* than that!

- **Revolve everything around Christ.** A Jesus-centered youth ministry gives teenagers the opportunity to see, hear, feel, and explore Jesus in every aspect of their lives. Jesus becomes something more real to them when Christ is the center of your *logos*. After all, the Bible tells us he IS the Logos (John 1:1)!

DIVINE ANTICIPATION STRATEGIES FOR PARENTS

Mothers and fathers can be your best allies or your worst enemies. However, much of the time they're simply indifferent. They drop their kids off and wave goodbye—and then never pay a whiff of attention to what's going on down in the youth room.

Ethos

- **Encourage trust in the Holy Spirit.** Appealing to God's credibility over our own is one way of letting parents know that we embrace the power of the Holy Spirit in our ministries. Letting go of our agendas and personal control is an act of faith that taps deeply into our emotions. In a spirit of humility, challenge moms and dads to expect the Holy Spirit to enable loving relationships to form in your youth group.

Pathos

- **Wash parents' feet.** Literally and figuratively. When Jesus washed the feet of his disciples, he demonstrated the power of servanthood. He also gave them a taste of what happens when we anticipate God reaching into our lives. You can do the same for parents in a variety of ways.

  One way is to wash their feet—literally. Invite them to a parent meeting where you plan to review what you've been experiencing in youth group. Then, in an act of love and divine anticipation, wash moms' and dads' feet, one at a time. You will make an unforgettable emotional impact as you illustrate the spirit of your youth ministry.

Logos

- **Get parents to share God Sightings, too.** Tell parents when you and their kids see God at work in your everyday lives. And then make it a regular practice to encourage parents to share their God Sightings. Amazing things will happen: Parents will instantly become God Sighting role models for their kids. Parents will begin to understand how their children are seeing how God works. And you'll give moms and dads a powerful view of what your ministry is really all about.

CHAPTER 3

*Misconceptions,
Mistakes, and
Revelations
About Communication*

THE SKINNY ON

COMMUNICATION

7 MYTHS ABOUT COMMUNICATION

MYTH #1: INFORMATION IS COMMUNICATION. In other words, what you teach is more important than how it's received.

It doesn't matter how masterfully talented we are at flowing golden rivers of wisdom out of our praise-holes. Nor does it matter how precise or extensive our theology lessons are. People don't grow into a relationship with God by merely hearing about it Sunday after Sunday. They have to experience it for themselves.

When it comes to communicating the power of God's Word, it's essential that we provide meaningful experiences that help teenagers see firsthand how God can transform their lives. No one learns to drive by simply reading a vehicle owner's manual. They have to get behind the wheel. The same is true for growing in faith. People have to try it for themselves, practice it, stumble through it, feel it, and even show others how it's done. Our magical words and profound knowledge aren't enough. Ever.

MYTH #2: EFFECTIVE COMMUNICATION ALWAYS BRINGS ABOUT CHANGE. To put it another way: If teenagers aren't changing, we're not communicating effectively.

There are a lot of factors that can determine whether someone is responsive to what we're trying to tell them. They may disagree with us. They may be distracted by more significant things going on in their lives. They may be biologically or chemically unable to absorb our message at the moment (they could be too tired or they might be affected by medication). Or, frankly, they may simply not like us and our finely trimmed soul patches.

It's tempting to blame communication for conflicts or a lack of influence. But keep in mind that a wide number of variables can affect our communication, no matter how healthy it may be. The key thing to remember is that communication in ministry is a living, ongoing process with multiple opportunities to share and be heard. Sometimes it can take months or years to make a meaningful connection.

MYTH #3: LOGIC AND FACTS ARE PERSUASIVE. Logic may be the truest truth in the world. And facts are facts, period. But study after study has shown that people are rarely swayed by certainties and rationality. *Logos* needs *pathos* and *ethos*.

This can be a challenge in Christian ministry. We try to convey the TRUTH about the gospel. And if people would just accept the truth, then their eyes would be opened and they would see how much their lives would be better with Jesus at the center.

Unfortunately, it doesn't work that way in real life. The truth WILL set you free...but not just because you tell it to me. People aren't moved by facts; they're moved by acts...of love.

Love is the most persuasive force in the world. When we focus our time on loving youth, their parents, and the other people in our ministries, only then can they be won over.

MYTH #4: 93 PERCENT OF COMMUNICATION IS NONVERBAL. You've probably heard this numerous times over the years. But while it's frequently cited, that figure is based on a certain type of communication (deciphering attitudes), and is not at all a universal principle. We hear it a lot so we think it's true. But it ain't.

If it were true, we wouldn't need subtitles when we watch foreign films. Somehow we'd manage to understand 93 percent of what's going on, even though we don't understand a word they're saying. When you talk with people who speak a foreign language you don't know, do you understand 93 percent of what they're telling you? Me neither.

Sometimes it can seem like adults and teens speak a different language. (It's so totes adorbs when that happens, doe.) Culturally, we're quite different from our younger friends, and those differences don't translate as fluidly as we might think they do. It would be a mistake to expect our nonverbals to do nearly all the heavy lifting in connecting with kids.

In addition, people have a variety of learning styles and types of intelligences. The aural-oriented person is much more likely to remember what you said than a visual person who only thinks in pictures. The 93 percent recipe just doesn't fit the mold for the majority of disparate communication strengths and weaknesses.

Besides all that, reducing all our communication efforts to an overly simple formula ignores the fact that our connections with other people take place under countless kinds of circumstances. A brief, heated argument is nothing like a prolonged smoochfest between lovers. The same goes for giving directions to a stranger, baking cookies with your grandmother, or praying with a suicidal teenager. To think that our words account for only 7 percent of life's most meaningful conversations is a misguided notion. Life isn't a formula; let's not live it that way.

MYTH #5: COMMUNICATION REQUIRES IMITATION.
While many in ministry strive to be "relevant," they often misinterpret "relevant" as adapting to their audience and becoming as much like them as possible. So we see grown adults trying to act like teenagers. The result is cringe-worthy.

Leadership fails when leaders try to be cool or just one of the guys (or girls). It doesn't work because they lose their credibility. They're not fooling anyone, and instead they parade an ironic farce of themselves.

Empathy is not the same as imitation.

When building relationships and loving others, we want to relate to each other, to regard each other with respect and appreciation, and to view each other as equals before God. Healthy communication gets derailed when we try to become the other person rather than understand each other. Big difference.

MYTH #6: A MESSAGE SENT IS A MESSAGE RECEIVED.
We have a tendency to think that just because we said something, the other person should have heard it. Most parents fall into this trap at some point. How many times have we said to our kids, "I TOLD you to _____. Why don't you ever listen to me?!" Many of us are also guilty of using this misconception as a passive aggressive weapon against others. "I told him _____, but I guess he didn't listen. I did all I could."

Healthy communication doesn't work that way.
This myth falls under the "assumption" category.
Communication is a complex and multifarious endeavor, and assumptions are, in the words of actor Henry Winkler, "the termites of relationships."[7]

MYTH #7: COMMUNICATION WILL SOLVE ALL YOUR PROBLEMS. Sometimes even our best attempts at effective communication can get us nowhere—or worse. We might think that if we just say the right thing, or tell the right story, or ask the right questions, things will invariably improve. Sometimes we even think that MORE communication will eventually make things better. It usually won't. Problems are inevitable and endless.

The converse to that is also a myth: Communication is not the cause of all problems. To point the finger at communication—especially a perceived lack of communication—is kind of lazy, and often misses the root of the issue.

THE 7 DEADLY COMMUNICATION SINS

OK, "sins" is probably a bit strong. But it made a good subhead. Anyway, these are things you should never, ever do when you communicate in youth ministry.

1. **Saying one thing and doing another.** On the surface, this is basic hypocrisy. But when communicating from a place of trust, leadership, or authority, its potential for real harm boils much deeper.

2. **Believing the message is more important than the people.** For many of us, this is a "no duh." But, sadly, this communication transgression happens rather frequently in today's churches.

3. **Answering everything with certainty.** (In other words, being a know-it-all.) "Oh, that's not me!" is the first thing most of us say. But hold on a minute. How often do we tell the kids in our ministries that we *don't* have a good answer to some of their toughest questions? I know a lot of good-hearted folks in ministry leadership roles who, in essence, pretend to be omniscient. They always have an explanation for everything, even when they obviously don't know what they're talking about. Hey, I've done it myself more times than I can count.

   The fact is, we have faith because we *don't* know everything. We don't have all the answers, so we trust God to guide us through the fog.

4. **Trying to impress, rather than express.** The moment we let the "show" get in the way of our efforts to connect with others is the moment we stop being effective. It's natural to want to look good in front of others, but ministry never was and never should be about the quality of our performance.

5. **Stifling two-way communication.** Few of us would say we're the most important person in the room. But that's exactly what happens when we spend the bulk of our time preaching, teaching, or sermonizing in one form or another. I have yet to meet a kid who loves to sit and listen to someone prattle on for 45 minutes. (Studies show that people never make it past a few minutes.[8]) They'd rather have a conversation.

6. **Relying primarily on one form of communication.** People receive and process information in a broad spectrum of ways. So the typical worship/sermon/Bible study method of church and youth groups only reaches a small minority of the people in your sphere of impact.

   When we stick to the "standard" forms of communicating in leadership, we're essentially treating everyone as if they're spongy clones; we expect them to soak up everything we say and let their hearts be transformed. We have a preconceived idea of how each teen should respond to our life-changing message, and then we shine our spotlights on the one or two who pretend they did.

7. **Assuming anything.** This isn't so much a sin as it's a major stumbling block of communicating. There are LOTS of things we shouldn't assume. Here are a few:

- That people know the Bible stories we're referring to.

- That people understand our Christian jargon.

- That people will remember anything we tell them.

- That people will relate to us.

- That people are listening to us.

- That people believe the same way we do.

- That people who don't believe as we do are wrong.

    Granted, it's difficult not to assume a great many things in our everyday lives. I assume my computer will turn on when I push the button. I assume this salad will not make me sick if I eat it. I assume no one at church will throw a hymnal at me if I sing off-key. But when it comes to communication, the less we assume, the greater our chances of connection with people on a more meaningful level.

Dishonorable mention: Speaking for God. Alas, this abominable practice happens on a regular basis in ministry, across every denomination and every part of the country.

When I was in high school, I had a T-shirt with a sketch of two little monsters on it. They were just cute, harmless, little toothy creatures, not unlike the trolls you'd see in Norwegian folklore. One Sunday, an adult in my church took me aside and said that God told him the little monster illustrations were pictures of actual demons—and strongly suggested that I burn my T-shirt. I nodded politely, thanked him for the heads-up, and then prayed about it. God didn't give me any warnings. God's Spirit didn't pierce my conscience. I concluded that the illustrations were harmless. And they were.

That experience itself was harmless, as well. But I've had other encounters that weren't so innocuous. One time a Christian leader told me that God didn't approve of my haircut. Another faithful authority in my life told me that God would never want me to go to a liberal arts college. And I can remember one particularly troubling occasion when a church leader informed me that God said I was covered in a "spirit of compression," whatever that meant.

Every day, kids are being told by the religious authorities in their lives that God said this or that, even though most of it is entirely extra-biblical. Some of it is benign, and a small amount of it would be considered nefarious, but I think the majority of it is, at best, misguiding, misleading, and counterproductive.

Whenever I hear someone say things like, "God told me to tell you..." or "God doesn't approve of your..." or "God wants you to...," I shut them out. I implore you to let God speak for himself through his Word and through his Spirit. Unless you're quoting Scripture, I'll just assume you're making things up.

➲ A YOUTH WORKER'S PERSPECTIVE *Jeffrey Wallace*

I get so frustrated with "prophecy-lying"! The Word of God is more than enough, and it does not need you or me to add anything to it or take anything away from it. I strongly encourage you not to speak for God, but allow God, through the Holy Spirit, to speak through you. As a communicator it is very easy for us to give in to the temptation to submit to our flesh. However, that is dangerous for us and for our ministries, and we should always stay far away from that because, I believe, it leads us outside of the will of God—and our efforts cannot be blessed.

THE ART OF MISUNDERSTANDING

It's an inevitable outcome of much of our communication: We WILL be misunderstood.

Do your teenagers ever write social networking posts about what you shared with them during one of your youth group sessions? Chances are good that some of them will share things you never said. A couple of them will probably even post something that contradicts what you said, giving you all the credit (or the blame).

It's not that you weren't clear, or that they didn't hear you properly. Misunderstanding happens. A LOT. We humans are rather adept at getting the details mixed up and twisted around. We should probably consider calling it something else entirely, because it's not always strictly misunderstanding. How about "multi-understanding"?

Some Christians might be uncomfortable with this line of thinking. After all, as Christ-followers we hold to one "truth." Yet while we firmly believe in the complete truth of Jesus Christ, many other things in life are open to interpretation. (The gray areas.) Our individual responses to God and his love vary as widely as our personalities. So although we have our theological non-negotiables, we also have heaps of fluid areas in which we slosh about and get uncomfortably wet and sometimes get splashed in the eyes.

Misunderstanding—or, if you please, multi-understanding—becomes an essential ingredient of the art of communication. Teenagers will hear our words and stories and, without fail, *form their own meaning.* This is a foundational function of communication, it's unavoidable, and it happens in virtually every human encounter. The level of misunderstanding can vary greatly, but it's there in some form or another. Oftentimes those misunderstandings can even be more meaningful than we intended.

Sometimes we even contradict ourselves, usually without realizing it. I wouldn't be surprised if somewhere over the course of this book I've contradicted myself. It happens to the best and worst of us. But we shouldn't expect communication to cure us of that tendency. Instead, communication allows us to expose our humanity and—mistakes and all—work through the meaning together.

You can count on misunderstanding. You can count on it happening, and you can count on it providing surprising and sometimes deeper meaning for the teenagers in your ministry. Maybe we need to be clearer. Maybe we need to repeat ourselves. Maybe we need to repeat ourselves. And maybe sometimes we need to come to grips with the possibility that we should be misunderstood. (Chew on that one for a minute or two.)

THE MAGIC OF LISTENING

Ministry, like relationships, is meant to be a two-way experience. Listening, therefore, is an indispensible function of effective ministry.

I'm as guilty as anyone when it comes to solving instead of listening. In my experience, most youth workers I know (and lead pastors, too) always have a well-thought-out, sage response to every person's story. They've got the perfect Scripture, timely anecdote, or wise resolution for every problem under the sun. Sure, solving people's problems can be an essential part of ministry. People want answers. But more than that, they need empathy and emotional support. They need to be heard.

Listening, unfortunately, is a skill that few people get training for. Business professionals and academic practitioners point to listening as one of the most important skills in their fields. But only 1.5 percent of business journal articles ever cover the topic of being an effective listener.[9] And less than 2 percent of people ever receive any formal education or training on listening skills and techniques.[10] Listening is central to healthy communication, yet we spend little to no time learning how to do it effectively.

It happens in the medical field, too. One study found that 7 times out of 10, doctors interrupt patient interviews within 18 seconds of the patient beginning to speak. In three out of four of those interviews, the patient never stated their real reason for visiting the doctor.[11] Another study found that two-thirds of malpractice cases were linked to poor communication, and that medical professionals with better communication skills were less likely to be sued.[12]

Things are no better in churches. The top two reasons people cite for not wanting to go to church[13] are rooted in a lack of listening. The top reason, "I feel judged," comes from a place of not being heard. When we see someone who's dressed inappropriately, or comes across as cold and distant, or somehow doesn't fit our mold, we tend to judge them based on those impressions. But when we listen to their stories and discover the journey they've been on, we find ourselves able to empathize and understand them. We're much less likely to judge.

The other top reason people say they don't want to go to church? "I don't want to be lectured." Obviously, that doesn't involve listening skills at all—at least on the part of the church. People—teens included—don't want to be talked to; they want to be talked *with*. Church is typically not the place they go to find meaningful conversation, which is also to say it's not the place they go to find meaningful relationships. As a youth leader, how much listening do you do on a typical Sunday morning?

By every definition I can find in the Bible, the church is supposed to be first and foremost a haven for relationships—not an academic institution, not a silo of isolation, and certainly not a theater where people come, sit, and enjoy the God show. Those relationships can only thrive in a vibrant culture of listening.

Think about all your closest relationships. How would you feel if your best friends, partner, and co-workers only ever tried to solve your problems? How much would you value your loved ones if they always tried to explain away your frustrations through Scripture and sage advice? What would you do if none of your closest friends ever simply listened to you and empathized with you?

People, especially teenagers, aren't looking for answers, explanations, or solutions. We may have the most astute answers, exceptional explanations, and smart solutions on the planet, but often that's not what teenagers are searching for. They simply want to be heard—truly heard. That's it.

"Don't try to fix it. I just need you to listen."

You can find a brilliant example of this in the short video called "It's Not About the Nail." You can watch it at this Vimeo link: http://vimeo.com/66753575

So, read through the following tips for being a better listener. Pick ONE to try this week in each of your conversations:

- **Repeat what you hear another person say.** Paraphrase it in your own words. Say, "So what I hear you saying is that...."

- **While you're listening, don't be thinking about what you're going to say next (often called the "rebuttal tendency").** We speak at a rate of about 125-250 words per minute, but we can think at a rate of up to 500 words per minute.[14] That means you'll have plenty of time to think about what you're going to say AFTER you've heard the speaker talk.

- **Ask follow-up questions.** Dig for relevant details (without being pushy or invasive).

- **Suppress your inner critic.** Are you responding to the speaker or what the speaker is saying? We have a tendency in our society to criticize the speaker rather than what the speaker says. It's essential to make sure our criticisms, answers, and responses focus on what's said, rather than aiming our criticism at the person. Imagine what a different world it would be if we stopped

being trolls and cutting people down personally
for their opinions and instead had an open,
respectful dialogue about the topic.

- **Don't assume you're a better listener than
you really are.** Expect to have to work at it.
Make it a habit to practice these listening skills
every time you engage in conversation.

CALIBRATING OUR EXPECTATIONS

When we say "Hi!" to someone, we expect, not
unreasonably, that person to say "Hi!" back. It's the
simplest and most commonly accepted way to measure
the success of that particular attempt at communication.
When we don't get that standard response ("Hi!" back),
we immediately make silent mental judgments. *Did they
hear me? Do they not speak English? Maybe they don't like
me. What a jerk!*

(Sometimes, if you're like me, saying "Hi!" isn't always
quite so simple. Sometimes, if you're like me, your words
get a little mixed up on their way from your brain to the
edge of your lips, and a simple "How's it going?" comes
out sounding like some kind of Precambrian gibberish:
"Hoober doring?" But anyway.)

Saying "Hi!" is an elementary example. Possible responses become much less predictable in more complex situations. Here's a list of questions, starting with ones that have the simplest expected responses down to the ones with the most unpredictable potential reactions:

- Is it raining?

- May I borrow your umbrella?

- Why are you all wet?

- Do you like the rain?

- I know it's raining, but can you help me jumpstart my car?

- When was the last time you got caught in the rain?

- Why does the rain always make you cry?

- What do you think it's like to die alone in the rain?

- Why did God make it rain today?

That last question is a doozy. Why? Because there's no right answer. We can't know why God made it rain, if indeed he was actually responsible for said rainstorm. There may have been 1,000 people praying for rain and

1,000 other people praying for no rain. Theological arguments aside, this last question is significant for at least three reasons: (1) It's difficult to predict the outcome of that conversation; (2) it's even more difficult to know what kinds of meaning people will draw from that conversation; and (3) it's nearly impossible to know the impact the conversation had on one's spiritual growth or transformation.

When we communicate in ministry, we usually have expectations about what the response should be. In general, we look for positive results—perhaps some laughs, a tear or two, some very sincere and earnest prayers, or, ideally, teenagers who publically make a major life commitment to God's kingdom.

There's nothing wrong with those expectations—except using them as the measure for your success. There can really be only one true measure for success in ministry: *Did you love them?* If the answer was yes, then mission accomplished. Sure, that love can take a million different forms in a billion different scenarios, but that's what you're striving to do. When we let the expectation of specific RESULTS dictate our progress, our efforts at communication lose their sincerity and effectiveness.

> **"The most powerful words in English are, 'Tell me a story.'"**
> —PAT CONROY, *MY READING LIFE*[15]

ENDNOTES

[1] James C. Christensen, Personal Illuminations Vol. 1: Imagination, (Salt Lake City, UT: Shadow Mountain, 2000), 30.

[2] sethgodin.typepad.com/seths_blog/2013/03/communication-is-a-path-not-an-event.html

[3] George Gallup Jr. and D. Michael Lindsay, *Surveying the Religious Landscape* (Dalton, GA: Morehouse Group, 1999). This book was also sourced in Thom and Joani Schultz's book *Why Nobody Wants to Go to Church Anymore.*

[4] While Aristotle doesn't specifically use these three words, they're referenced as concepts throughout the text. See hbr.org/2013/01/three-elements-of-great-communication-according/

[5] Clay Shirky, *Here Comes Everybody: The Power of Organizing Without Organizations* (New York, NY: Penguin Press, 2008), 50.

[6] Chip Heath and Dan Heath, *Made to Stick: Why Some Ideas Survive and Others Die* (New York, NY: Random House, 2008), 88.

[7] thinkexist.com/quotation/assumptions_are_the_termites_of_relationships-i/209113.html

[8] See telegraph.co.uk/news/health/news/3522781/Stress-of-modern-life-cuts-attention-spans-to-five-minutes.html; and psychminds.com/is-the-internet-destroying-our-attentions-span/; and fortune.com/2013/07/10/giving-a-speech-conquer-the-five-minute-attention-span/

[9] L.R. Smeltzer, "Emerging Questions and Research Paradigms in Business Communication Research," The Journal of Business Communication, (30: 1993), 181-198.

[10] forbes.com/sites/glennllopis/2013/05/20/6-effective-ways-listening-can-make-you-a-better-leader/2/

[11] J. Lee, "10 Ways to Communicate Better With Patients," Review of Ophthalmology (2000), 38-42.

[12] G.B. Hickson, P.B. Clayton, P.E. Giethen, and F.A. Sloan, "Factors That Prompted Families to File Medical Malpractice Claims Following Perinatal Injuries," Journal of American Medical Association (267: 1992), 2359-1363.

[13] Research about the top reasons people don't want to attend church can be found in Thom and Joani Schultz's book *Why Nobody Wants to Go to Church Anymore* (Loveland, CO: Group Publishing, 2013).

[14] See uwyo.edu/math/_files/docs/improve%20your%20 listening.html; and extension.missouri.edu/p/CM150

[15] Pat Conroy, *My Reading Life* (New York, NY: Knopf Doubleday Publishing Group, 2010), 301.